ORTRAITS O

★ ★ ★ ★ ★ ★ ★ ★ ★ ★ ★ ★

OKLAHOMA

by Jonatha A. Brown

GARETH**STEVENS**
GS
P U B L I S H I N G
A Member of the WRC Media Family of Companies

Please visit our web site at: **www.garethstevens.com**
For a free color catalog describing Gareth Stevens Publishing's
list of high-quality books and multimedia programs, call
1-800-542-2595 (USA) or 1-800-387-3178 (Canada).
Gareth Stevens Publishing's fax: (414) 332-3567.

Library of Congress Cataloging-in-Publication Data

Brown, Jonatha A.
   Oklahoma / Jonatha A. Brown.
     p. cm. — (Portraits of the states)
   Includes bibliographical references and index.
   ISBN 0-8368-4672-9 (lib. bdg.)
   ISBN 0-8368-4691-5 (softcover)
   1. Oklahoma—Juvenile literature. I. Title. II. Series.
   F694.3.B75   2006
   976.6—dc22   2005044480

This edition first published in 2006 by
Gareth Stevens Publishing
A Member of the WRC Media Family of Companies
330 West Olive Street, Suite 100
Milwaukee, WI 53212 USA

This edition copyright © 2006 by Gareth Stevens, Inc.

Editorial direction: Mark J. Sachner
Project manager: Jonatha A. Brown
Editor: Catherine Gardner
Art direction and design: Tammy West
Picture research: Diane Laska-Swanke
Indexer: Walter Kronenberg
Production: Jessica Morris and Robert Kraus

Picture credits: Cover, pp. 4, 15, 17, 18, 20, 22, 24, 25, 26, 27 © John Elk III;
p. 5 Oklahoma Tourism & Recreation Dept.; pp. 6, 9 © MPI/Getty Images;
p. 8 © Kean Collection/Getty Images; p. 10 © Hulton Archive/Getty Images;
p. 12 © Bob Daemmrich/AFP/Getty Images; p. 29 © Dilip Vishwanat/Getty Images

Printed in the United States of America

1 2 3 4 5 6 7 8 9 10 09 08 07 06

CONTENTS

★ ★

Words that are defined in the Glossary appear
in **bold** the first time they are used in the text.

On the Cover: The Wichita Mountains provide a safe habitat for many
kinds of wildlife in southwestern Oklahoma.

Introduction

If you could visit Oklahoma, what would you like to do? Visit a Native American powwow? Visit the Rodeo Hall of Fame? Hike in the mountains and look for bald eagles? This state has so much to offer that you may have trouble deciding what to do first.

Oklahoma has busy cities and rugged mountains. Ranches cover large areas of land, and oil wells rise up from flat plains. The state has a rich history, too. You can learn about it at many museums and historical sites.

The people of Oklahoma are friendly. They invite you to join them at a rodeo or a festival. So, come to Oklahoma and have a good time!

Native festivals take place all over Oklahoma. They often feature costumed dancers like these.

The state flag of Oklahoma.

OKLAHOMA FACTS

- Became the 46th State: November 16, 1907
- Population (2004): 3,523,553
- Capital: Oklahoma City
- Biggest Cities: Oklahoma City, Tulsa, Norman, Lawton
- Size: 68,667 square miles (177,847 square km)
- Nickname: The Sooner State
- State Tree: Redbud
- State Flower: Mistletoe
- State Animal: American buffalo
- State Bird: Scissor-tailed flycatcher

History

People have lived in Oklahoma for thousands of years. The first people to live in this part of the country were Native Americans. They roamed from place to place as they hunted buffalo.

Europeans Arrive

In 1541, a group of Spaniards reached the area. Francisco Vásquez de Coronado and his men were looking for gold. They left without finding it. Other explorers from Spain followed. They did not stay long.

More than one hundred years passed. French traders arrived. They traded with the Natives for furs. They sent the furs to Europe.

In the 1700s, both France and Spain wanted to own this region. First one

Hernando de Soto was one of the Spaniards who explored parts of what is today Oklahoma. He reached the area in 1541.

country and then the other claimed it. In 1803, the United States bought a big piece of land from France. The deal was known as the Louisiana Purchase. Most of Oklahoma was included in this deal.

Then, more traders and explorers came. In 1817, a Frenchman set up a trading post. He built it on the spot where Salina now lies. It was the first long-lasting **settlement** in Oklahoma.

Indian Territory

In the early 1800s, many Native Americans still lived in the southeastern United States. The settlers wanted the land. They did not want the Natives there. The U.S. government decided to make the Natives move west. First, however, it had to have a place to put them.

The government began making deals with Natives in eastern Oklahoma. It bought lots of land from them. This land became known as Indian **Territory**. Now, the government had a place to send Natives from the East Coast.

In 1830, the U.S. Army began forcing Natives to leave their homes in the Southeast. Many did not want to go. Fighting broke out, but the Army won in the end. Over the next fifty

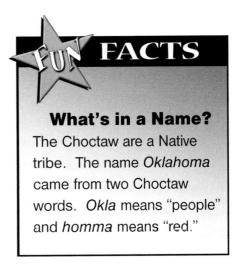

FACTS

What's in a Name?
The Choctaw are a Native tribe. The name *Oklahoma* came from two Choctaw words. *Okla* means "people" and *homma* means "red."

years, more than sixty tribes were forced to move to Indian Territory.

Other Natives already lived on this land. They did not always welcome the new Native people. The tribes fought with each other. They fought with the U.S. Army, too. This fighting went on for many years.

The Land Run

In the 1830s, Texas held a small strip of land that is now part of Oklahoma. Texas became a U.S. state in 1845. This brought the last bit of present-day Oklahoma under U.S. control.

In the mid-1800s, large parts of Oklahoma were known as "**Unassigned** Lands." The name meant that no Native tribes had been forced to live there.

IN OKLAHOMA'S HISTORY

The Trail of Tears

The Cherokee are a Native American tribe. They once lived in the southeastern United States. In 1838, the U.S. Army forced them to march to Oklahoma. The trip took 116 days. Food was scarce, and the weather grew cold. More than four thousand people died. This awful journey became known as the Trail of Tears.

In 1868, the U.S. Army attacked a group of Natives who were living along the Wasatch River. Dozens of men, women, and children died or were taken prisoner in this raid.

Few white people had settled in this region, either. The area was not officially open to settlement.

Many non-Native people wanted to move to this land. Finally, the government agreed to hold a "land run" in 1889. Huge crowds of people showed up. The U.S. Army held them back until a pistol was fired to signal the start of the run. Then, the people ran or rode as fast as they could to grab some land. By the end of the first day, this part of the country had about fifty thousand new **residents**. Oklahoma City and Guthrie sprung up overnight.

This is the brand new city of Guthrie. It is shown here just five days after the land run began in April 1889.

FUN FACTS

The Sooner State

The first land run was set for April 22, 1889, but some settlers did not want to wait. They sneaked in and claimed their land early. These people were known as "sooners." Later, Oklahoma became known as "the Sooner State."

IN OKLAHOMA'S HISTORY

Civil War

The United States fought the Civil War from 1861 until 1865. The North fought the South. Many Natives in Indian Territory were from the South. Some even owned slaves. These Natives sided with the South during the war. When the North won, it set the slaves free. It also punished the tribes that had sided with the South by taking away some of their land.

Life was not easy for most African Americans in Oklahoma in the early 1900s.

Most settlers became ranchers. Before long, huge herds of cattle roamed the land.

Two Territories

The Oklahoma Territory was set up in 1890. It included only the land that is now western Oklahoma. Indian Territory was separate. Only Natives could live there. Years earlier, the government had forced many Natives to leave their homes. It had made them move to Indian Territory. Now, white settlers were not content to let Natives have this land.

The U.S. government tried to make deals with the Natives. It offered to make them U.S. citizens. It offered to let them own small pieces of land. Then, the settlers would have the rest. The Natives agreed. In the end, they had even less land than they had before.

Indian Territory was opened for settlement in 1899. More land runs took place. Many settlers moved in. Soon, Natives made up less than 20 percent of the people in the territory.

The two territories were combined in 1907. In that year, they became the state of Oklahoma. Oil had been discovered on this land ten years before. Oil made some people rich. Ranching was still a good way to make a living, too.

Hard Times

In the 1920s, crop prices fell. Many people lost their jobs. It was a tough time for the people who lived in Oklahoma.

More oil was found near Oklahoma City in 1928. This brought jobs back to the state. Oklahoma became the country's top producer of oil. Life there was better for a short time.

Dust Bowl

In the 1930s, prices fell again. A **drought** hit the state at the same time. Without rain, crops failed. Much of the West, including

IN OKLAHOMA'S HISTORY

Murders and Race Riots

Many people in Oklahoma were out of work in the early 1920s. Some of them blamed African Americans for the problems. A powerful group of white men began killing blacks. This group was the Ku Klux Klan. They were not put in jail for their crimes. Tensions between the races grew. In 1921, African Americans in Tulsa **rioted**. Whole city blocks burned, and many people died.

On April 19, 1995, a bomb exploded at the Alfred P. Murrah Federal Building in Oklahoma City. It caused terrible damage. Many people died.

Oklahoma became known as "the Dust Bowl." Thousands of people moved away from the state. Many of them headed west to look for jobs on farms in California. These homeless people were known as "Okies."

Better Times

The drought ended in the late 1930s. Soon, crops were growing again. Even so, farming became less important. Oil became the top product.

In the 1960s, dams were built across rivers. The water behind the dams now provides power for many businesses in the state. These days, rising oil prices are helping the oil business. The people of Oklahoma are looking forward to a bright future.

IN OKLAHOMA'S HISTORY

Terrorist Attack

In 1995, a truck bomb exploded in Oklahoma City. The bomber was a man from another state. His bomb blew up the Alfred P. Murrah Federal Building. Almost 170 people died. Hundreds more were wounded. The people of the state were deeply shaken. They built a **memorial** to those who died.

12

Time Line

About 13,000 B.C.	The first Natives reach the area that is now Oklahoma.
1541	Francisco Vásquez de Coronado explores the area for Spain.
1817	The first lasting settlement is founded at Salina.
1830	The U.S. government starts forcing many tribes to move from the Southeast to eastern Oklahoma.
1834	The U.S. Congress officially sets up Indian Territory.
1889	The first "land run" takes place in western Oklahoma.
1890	Oklahoma Territory is created.
1897	The first big oil well is drilled in Oklahoma.
1907	Indian Territory and Oklahoma Territory are combined. They become the state of Oklahoma.
1921	Because of cruel treatment, African Americans riot in Tulsa. About three hundred people are killed.
1928	A huge oil field is found and drilling begins.
1995	A terrorist's bomb kills 168 people in Oklahoma City.
1999	About forty tornadoes hit Oklahoma. They cause great damage.

People

Oklahoma is a large state in land area. Yet it has a fairly small **population**. About 3.5 million people live there. The largest city is Oklahoma City. About one-third of the people in the state live in this city or nearby.

Many Backgrounds

Over 75 percent of the people in this state are white. Quite a few can trace their families back to the early settlers. Many of these settlers came from Kansas,

Hispanics: In the 2000 U.S. Census, 5.2 percent of the people in Oklahoma called themselves Latino or Hispanic. Most of them or their relatives came from places where Spanish is spoken. They may come from different racial backgrounds.

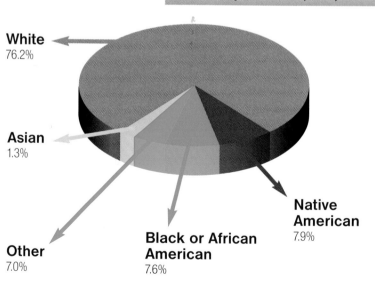

The People of Oklahoma

Total Population 3,523,553

White
76.2%

Asian
1.3%

Other
7.0%

Black or African American
7.6%

Native American
7.9%

Percentages are based on the 2000 Census.

Arkansas, and Texas. Others were from Europe.

Today, few people move to Oklahoma from other countries. Most of these people come from Mexico. Others come from Vietnam, India, and other places in the world.

Almost 8 percent of the people in the state are Native Americans. They belong to more than sixty tribes. A few tribes have lived in this state for hundreds of years.

Oklahoma City got its start during the land run of 1889. It grew up along both sides of the North Canadian River. It is now the largest city and the capital of Oklahoma.

Others were forced to move to Oklahoma in the 1800s.

African Americans are the third-largest group in the state. Long ago, many black men and women came to this area as slaves. After the Civil War, the slaves were freed. Many freed slaves left the South and moved to

Famous People of Oklahoma

Wilma Mankiller

Born: November 18, 1945, Tahlequah, Oklahoma

Wilma Mankiller is a Native American. She belongs to the Cherokee tribe. She lived on a farm in Oklahoma when she was a small child. Her family moved to California while she was still young. She moved back to Oklahoma in the 1970s. There, Mankiller worked to help her people. She helped improve schools, health care, and housing. She became well known and well respected. In 1985, she became the chief of the Cherokee Nation. She is the first woman ever to become a Cherokee chief.

Oklahoma. They founded more than twenty towns.

Education and Religion

The first schools in the state opened in the mid-1800s. These schools were started by Native Americans who had been forced to the area from the East Coast. Some churches in the East set up more schools for Natives. Today, the state has a system of public schools.

The state's first public universities were set up in the 1890s. Today, Oklahoma has a number of colleges and universities. Some of them are funded by the state. Others are private schools.

Almost 90 percent of the people in the state are Christian. Many of them are Baptists, Methodists, and Catholics. Other people in the state practice different

faiths. A few are Jewish, Hindu, and Buddhist. Some practice Native religions.

Northeastern State University is in Tahlequah. Oklahoma's state university system has branches in several cities.

Famous People of Oklahoma

Woody Guthrie

Born: July 14, 1912, Okemah, Oklahoma

Died: October 3, 1967, Queens, New York

Woody Guthrie was born Woodrow Wilson Guthrie. He grew up to be a famous folk singer. One of his biggest hits was "This Land Is Your Land." He left Oklahoma during the drought of the 1930s. Like other "Okies," he drifted to California. There, he worked in the fields and wrote and sang songs. Some of his most famous songs were about the hard lives of people who work at low-paying jobs.

17

The Land

O klahoma is shaped like a cooking pot with a long handle. The handle comes out of the northwest corner of the state. This long, narrow part of the state is called the Panhandle.

Plains cover about two-thirds of Oklahoma. On the plains, the land is mostly flat or rolling. Many kinds of grasses grow there. Sagebrush and cactus grow in the driest areas. This land is good for farming and raising cattle. These open areas are home to many kinds of animals. Prairie dogs, rabbits, and coyotes are common. **Armadillos** live there, too. Most of

FUN FACTS

Riches under the Ground

Treasure lies under the ground in Oklahoma! The state is one of the top oil producers in the nation. It also has large coal deposits. Limestone, salt, granite, and lead are mined, too.

Black Mesa rises up from the plains. It is the highest point in the state.

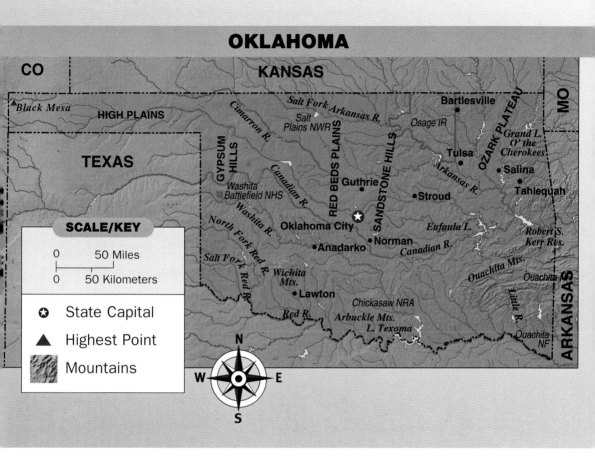

CO
KANSAS

Black Mesa
HIGH PLAINS

TEXAS

Salt Fork Arkansas R.
Salt
Plains NWR

Bartlesville

Osage IR

Grand L.
O' the
Cherokees

Tulsa

OZARK PLATEAU

MO

Salina

Tahlequah

GYPSUM HILLS

Cimarron R.

Canadian R.

Washita
Battlefield NHS
Washita R.

North Fork Red R.

Salt Fork Red R.

RED BEDS PLAINS

Guthrie

SANDSTONE HILLS

Stroud

Arkansas R.

Oklahoma City

Anadarko

Norman

Eufaula L.

Canadian R.

Robert S.
Kerr Res.

Wichita
Mts.

Lawton

Chickasaw NRA

Red R.

Arbuckle Mts.

L. Texoma

Ouachita Mts.

Little R.

Ouachita

Ouachita
NF

ARKANSAS

SCALE/KEY

0   50 Miles

0   50 Kilometers

⊗ State Capital

▲ Highest Point

   Mountains

N

W — E

S

the towns and cities in the state are also located in the plains region.

The highest point in the state is also on the plains. Black Mesa is 4,973 feet (1,516 meters) high. It is in the northwest corner of the Panhandle. Black Mesa is not a mountain. It is a big area of fairly flat land that is higher than the land around

it. This kind of land is called a **plateau**.

Along the Red River, the land is much lower. Swamps have formed in some places.

Highlands

Rugged hills and mountains can also be found in the state. The main mountain ranges are the Wichita, Arbuckle, and Ouachita

Mountains. They are in the southern part of the state. Oak and pine forests cover much of the Ouachitas and the land nearby.

The Gypsum Hills are in the west, and the Sandstone Hills are in the center. In the northeast is the Ozark Plateau. This is an area of wide, flat-topped hills with

steep sides. Forests cover much of this land. Oak and hickory trees grow there, too. Rivers run between the steep hills.

Major Rivers

Arkansas River
1,450 miles (2,333 km) long

Red River
1,018 miles (1,638 km) long

Canadian River
906 miles (1,458 km) long

The Wichita Mountains are lovely. Here, Elk Mountain rises above peaceful Treasure Lake.

Antelope live in these upland areas. Deer, elk, foxes, and many other animals can be found, too. The Wichita Mountains even have small herds of buffalo. They are protected by law.

Waterways

The Arkansas River is the biggest river in the state. Many smaller rivers flow into it. The Red River forms the state's southern border. All of the streams in the state drain into the Gulf of Mexico far to the south of Oklahoma.

Oklahoma has many lakes. The largest lakes are man made. They were created by dams that were built across rivers. Eufaula Lake is the biggest lake in the state.

Ducks and geese thrive along the waterways. Bass, carp, catfish, and sunfish are just a few of the fish that swim in the rivers and lakes.

Climate

The climate in Oklahoma is fairly warm. The southern part of the state gets the most heat and rain. Farmers in the south can grow crops about eight months out of the year. The western part of the state is much drier. Droughts sometimes hit the Panhandle.

FACTS

Twisters

Tornadoes are common in this state. In just one day in 2004, ten tornadoes touched down north of Oklahoma City. The whirling winds wrecked houses and tore trees out of the ground. The storms killed three people.

Economy

In the late 1800s, cattle ranching was the top business in Oklahoma. Oil was a big money maker, too. Today, both beef and oil are still produced in the state. Yet, other **industries** are even more important.

Service Jobs

As in most states, many people work in service jobs. Service workers have jobs that help other people. Some service workers are doctors and nurses. Others are teachers and car **mechanics**. People who work in hotels and restaurants are service workers, too.

Manufacturing and Energy

Manufacturing is also important. Many factories make electrical equipment.

Oil wells are a common sight in many parts of Oklahoma.

Some make computer parts. Others make machines for building and for drilling oil.

Oklahoma is still a leading oil state. It also produces lots of natural gas. Pipelines carry most of the gas to other states. The rest is used to make electricity in Oklahoma. Coal is used to make electricity, too. Large amounts of coal are mined in this state.

Farming

Farming is not as important in Oklahoma as it once was. Even so, three-fourths of the land in the state is used for farming and ranching. Beef cattle are the biggest farm product. Chickens and pigs are raised in Oklahoma, too. Wheat is the biggest field crop. Hay, cotton, and corn are other widely grown crops.

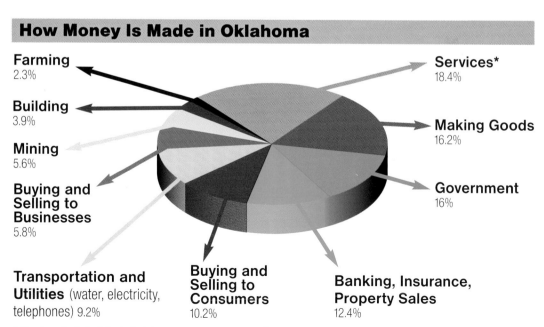

How Money Is Made in Oklahoma

Farming
2.3%

Building
3.9%

Mining
5.6%

Buying and Selling to Businesses
5.8%

Services*
18.4%

Making Goods
16.2%

Government
16%

Transportation and Utilities (water, electricity, telephones) 9.2%

Buying and Selling to Consumers
10.2%

Banking, Insurance, Property Sales
12.4%

* Services include jobs in hotels, restaurants, auto repair, medicine, teaching, and entertainment.

Government

The capital of Oklahoma is Oklahoma City. The leaders of the state work there. The state government has three parts. They are the executive, legislative, and judicial branches.

Executive Branch

The executive branch carries out the state's laws. The governor is the leader of this branch. A lieutenant governor helps. Other officials also work for the governor.

For many years, the state capitol did not have a dome on top. The dome was added in 2001.

Legislative Branch

The Oklahoma Legislature has two parts. They are the Senate and the House of Representatives. They work together to make laws for the state.

Guthrie was the capital of the state from 1907 to 1910. The Logan County Courthouse served as the capitol building.

Judicial Branch

Judges and courts make up the judicial branch. Judges and courts may decide whether people who have been **accused of** committing crimes are guilty.

Local Government

Oklahoma has seventy-seven counties. Each is run by a team of three people. There are almost six hundred cities and towns in the state, too. Most of them are run by a mayor or a city manager and a city council.

Many Native groups govern themselves. The Cherokee Nation is one of these groups. It has its headquarters in Tahlequah.

OKLAHOMA'S STATE GOVERNMENT

Executive		Legislative		Judicial	
Office	**Length of Term**	**Body**	**Length of Term**	**Court**	**Length of Term**
Governor	4 years	Senate (48 members)	4 years	Supreme (9 justices)	6 years
Lieutenant Governor	4 years	House of Representatives (101 members)	2 years	Appeals (17 judges)	6 years

Things to See and Do

Oklahoma is a great place to enjoy the outdoors. It has more than fifty state parks. Beavers Bend is in the Ouachita Mountains. You can pitch a tent there and spend a few days in the wild. At **Alabaster** Caverns, you can explore a big cave. The walls of the cave are made of a lovely white stone known as alabaster. Five kinds of bats live there.

The Salt Plains National Wildlife Refuge is a great spot for bird watching. Bald eagles soar overhead. You may see cranes and pelicans, too.

Special lighting brings out the beauty of a cave at Alabaster Caverns.

Native Ways

Each year in August, Native Americans hold a festival in Anadarko. It lasts one week. People who go to the festival enjoy Native foods, music, dancing, and a rodeo. Tahlequah, Stroud, and Oklahoma City also host Native powwows.

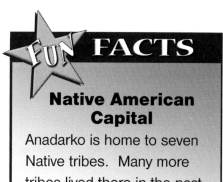

Many museums in the state focus on Native American history. Some of the best are in Anadarko, Tahlequah, and Bartlesville. They display tepees, blankets, and more.

In Tahlequah, you can visit the Cherokee Heritage Center. There, you can see how some Natives lived before Europeans arrived.

Historic Sites and Museums

The state has many historic sites. Fort Smith is one place to learn about life in Indian Territory. Washita Battlefield is interesting, too. It was the site of a

Famous People of Oklahoma

Mickey Mantle

Born: October 20, 1931, Spavinaw, Oklahoma

Died: August 13, 1995, Dallas, Texas

Mickey Mantle was a great baseball player. He played for the New York Yankees in the mid-1900s. He was an amazing hitter. In 1956, he had the best batting average in baseball. That same year, he hit more home runs and batted in more runs than any other player in the American League. Mantle was voted the Most Valuable Player in the league three times. He helped his team win the World Series seven times during his career.

bloody clash between the U.S. Army and a group of Natives in 1868.

Several museums are in Oklahoma City. One is the National Cowboy and Western Heritage Museum. It includes the Rodeo Hall of Fame. If you are a rodeo fan, be sure not to miss it! For fun with science, visit the Kirkpatrick Science and Air Space Museum. Both kids and adults like its hands-on exhibits.

The city of Tulsa also has fine museums. Native art is displayed at the Gilcrease Museum. The Philbrook Museum of Art is known for paintings from Europe and Asia.

Sports

Dozens of rodeos take place in Oklahoma every year.

Some are just for young people. Others are for **pros**. The International Finals Rodeo is held in Oklahoma City. It is one of the best rodeos in the country.

People in Oklahoma like team sports. College football games draw big crowds. The Sooners are one of the state's best teams. They play for the University of Oklahoma. Their fans were thrilled when they won the Orange Bowl in 2001.

FUN FACTS

Ride 'Em, Cowboy!

Every winter, fifty of the best bull riders in the land head for Guthrie. There, they compete in a Bullnanza. The contest lasts two days. Each person in the contest tries to ride bulls without getting bucked off. The rider who stays on a bull the longest wins money and prizes.

The University of Oklahoma Sooners charge down the field in a fierce game against the University of Colorado Buffaloes.

accused of — blamed for

alabaster — a milky white stone that has a soft sheen

armadillos — burrowing animals whose head and body have horny plates

drought — a long dry period without enough rain for crops to grow

industries — groups of businesses that offer the same type of product or service

manufacturing — making goods in factories

mechanics — people who fix broken machines

memorial — a statue or other thing that honors someone who has died

plains — large areas of flat or gently rolling land, usually with few trees

plateau — a large, flat area that is higher than the land around it

population — the number of people who live in a city, state, or other place

pros — people who play a sport for money; short for the word "professionals"

residents — the people who live in a place

rioted — acted as a wild mob that breaks things and causes trouble

settlement — a town that has recently been built

territory — an area that belongs to a country

unassigned — not yet set aside for a particular purpose

Books

Cherokee Indians. Native Peoples (series). Bill Lund
(Children's Press)

I Have Heard of a Land. Joyce Carol Thomas (Joanna Cotler)

Oklahoma. United States (series). Paul Joseph (Abdo)

*One April Morning: Children Remember the Oklahoma City
Bombing.* Nancy Lamb (HarperCollins)

S is for Sooner: An Oklahoma Alphabet. Devin Scillian
(Sleeping Bear Press)

*They Came from the Bronx: How the Buffalo Were Saved
from Extinction.* Neil Waldman (Boyds Mills)

Woody Guthrie: Poet of the People. Bonnie Christensen
(Random House)

Web Sites

Diamond R Ranch Web Page
www.nationalcowboymuseum.org/diamondr/index.html

Enchanted Learning: Oklahoma
www.enchantedlearning.com/usa/states/oklahoma/

Oklahoma Fun Facts
www.oklahoma.feb.gov/FEBKids/Funfacts.htm

Oklahoma Historical Society's Sites and Museums
www.ok-history.mus.ok.us/mas/maspage.htm

INDEX